Joys of Spring

SPRING CELEBRATIONS AROUND THE WORLD

by Heather Conrad

Lightport Books
PO Box 7112
Berkeley, CA 94707
Lightportbooks.org

Many thanks —

*to Kate Colwell, Ginny Orenstein, Bobbi Sloan, and Sandra Treacy
for their essential help with this project.*

© 2018 by Heather Conrad

All rights reserved. No part of this book may be reproduced in any form or by any means, electronic or mechanical, including photocopying, recording or by any information storage and retrieval system, without permission in writing from the Publisher. Inquiries should be addressed to Lightport Books, PO Box 7112, Berkeley, CA 94707

ISBN 978-0-9712425-9-3

The abstract wattle image in "Wattle Day" was inspired by the painting "Acacia Flower" by Mary Pitjara

Springtime

In springtime, I fly around the world to see people celebrating everywhere! The sun is shining and flowers are blooming. The Earth is coming back to life! The sunlit soil is warm and soft and people plant many seeds for food to grow.

I love to fly in the soft warm air and watch my feathered friends build their nests. Did you know people in different countries have spring parties with EGGS and SEEDS to remind them of new life? Many celebrate WOMEN and MOTHERS in honor of Mother Earth. There is dancing and music and the sound of drums. There are parties with FLOWERS and LIGHT from candles and bonfires to remind everyone of the joys of spring.

Come with me and I'll show you! Can you find the things I see?

Noruz

First I arrive in the Middle East. Three thousand years ago, Persian people named the first day of spring Noruz. It means New Day. Now Persia is called Iran, and I begin my spring journey here. I stay two weeks for all the parties! Everyone cleans their house and wears new clothes. I watch as they build bonfires outside. I'm surprised when people jump over them! This is the way they say good-bye to the old year and begin a brand new one. At the parties they eat special meals—healing spices, fruits, and eggs. There are glowing candles and sprouted seeds called *sabzeh* decorating the table in honor of new life. I love to watch the dancers and hear the tambourines and horns playing a joyful song of spring.

Passover

Now I fly west, to Egypt, which is a very old country in Africa. Three thousand years ago, the Jewish people were slaves there. One day, they escaped and traveled far away. Now, all over the world, Jewish people celebrate Passover every spring to remember their long journey to freedom. I watch a family and their friends share a special meal called a *Seder*. They have bitter herbs for a memory of the past, and fresh vegetables for hope for the future, and nuts and apples, an egg and lamb and wine. Each of these foods is a special reminder of what their ancestors went through. I listen to them read a book called the *Haggadah* that tells how they escaped slavery and began a new life.

Gelede

Now I fly south and west across Africa to where the Yoruba people live. I see they are planting their new crops. And they are starting their Gelede celebration as they have every spring for over 1,000 years. They are gathering in the center of the village. And the masquerade dance begins! Many dancers wear a mask of a woman's face, even though all the dancers are men! They do this to honor all mothers and creation. And some wear masks with snakes and birds to celebrate the power of women and new life. I watch the wonderful dances. Then I fly away, west again, and far across the ocean.

Kolla Raymi Killa

I see land! It is South America, and I fly south to it, and high, high up into the Andes mountains. I rest a long time here after flying so far. This place is on the other side of the "equator"—that is an imaginary circle around the middle of the Earth. The equator divides Earth into halves called hemispheres. I am in the southern hemisphere now, where spring is in September! That is because Earth is closer to the sun at a different time here than it is in the North.

The Quechua people in the Andes of Peru call the first day of spring Kolla Raymi Killa. It is the time to plant seeds for new crops, and there is a fiesta! I see people placing many seeds in a circle as they honor *Kolla*—woman, and *Killa*—the moon, and the new life of spring. I watch all the people dressed in bright colors, making music and dancing. I love the sound of the flutes!

Wattle Day

From the mountains I fly high in the sky and all around the southern half of Earth, to Australia! Spring is in September here, too. Everyone celebrates Wattle Day. A wattle is a fuzzy yellow flower that blooms on acacia trees in springtime.

Aboriginal people have lived in Australia for over 60,000 years! And they have used the wattle tree for so many things. They gather seeds for food—and wood, leaves, bark, and roots in order to make medicines and tools, and musical instruments and colorful dyes.

Now all over Australia people celebrate the beautiful wattle on September 1st. I sit on a blossoming branch and watch people on "bushwalks"—that's a hike in the country. Some people wear yellow and green clothes to look like the wattle. And many plant new trees on this day to keep the lovely wattle growing every spring.

Sakura Matsuri

Now I fly due north, over the equator and far beyond, and I arrive in Japan! Here I rest a long, long time, until March, when it is springtime again in the North. The Japanese people celebrate spring for one whole month! It is called—Sakura Matsuri—the Cherry Blossom Festival. On the very first day people dress in costumes. And they make a drink from cherry blossoms called *sakura-yu*. I have a little taste of it and it is very good! Day after day, people have picnics and sing songs beneath flowering trees. I sit in a cherry tree and listen to one of their favorite songs. It is about blossoms that float like mist across mountains and towns, as far as you can see, and how they smell so sweet in the morning sun. Then I fly away, in the soft, light air.

Chun Fen

I fly to the west and soon I am in China. Here people celebrate March 21st, the first day of spring, with eggs! It is a custom that began 4,000 years ago. They have contests to see who can balance an egg on its end because if you can do it, you will have good luck in the future! I love to watch them try and try, and the children love to paint the eggs many colors.

In the countryside, people also celebrate by thanking birds—the geese who fly north every year in early spring and let farmers know it is time to plant. Also, the farmers ask the birds—"please don't eat our seeds!" And the farmers make sticky rice balls, so sweet and delicious, to feed to their cows to thank them for their hard work on the farm! Everyone is thankful for new life and the joys of spring.

Basant Panchami

Now I fly high, high to the west, and south over the Himalayan mountains! I land in the vast region of India and Pakistan. I discover so many people celebrating a glorious spring: Muslims, Hindus and Sikhs. Many wear bright yellow clothes. The Sufi Muslims honor the story of a holy man named Nizamuddin who was sad when his young nephew died. His friend brought him bright yellow mustard flowers to help him remember there is new life and joy. Hindu people honor the story of Saraswati, the mother of wisdom, art and music. And the Sikhs remember two hundred years ago when Maharaja Ranjit Singh began a tradition at the end of winter—flying kites in the wide blue sky! All celebrate new life on Basant Panchami, a time of music, dancing and joy. I watch the dancers flying about like the colorful kites in the sky.

Holi

I fly and fly over India because here, and in many lands where Hindu people live, there is a wonderful Festival of Colors in spring. It is called Holi and is a special day to celebrate goodness and light, the end of winter and the beginning of new life. It is a time to be with family and friends and celebrate each other, to forgive, and to laugh. There are visits and parties and everyone sprays brightly colored powders on everyone they meet! Friends and strangers—it is a time to play and have fun!

Easter Sunday

When I leave Asia, I fly a long time over Europe and then across the ocean to the Americas. In many places, I see Christian people celebrating Easter. Easter is always on the first Sunday after the full moon following March 21st. On Easter Sunday, Christian people remember the Bible story from 2,000 years ago when Jesus Christ came back to life after his death.

Now, I see a Christian family wearing their best new clothes to church and the church bells ring and ring! I see them with their friends, too, walking in parades and having parties with bunnies and baby chicks, and flowers and baskets and candies. Wait! There are little children looking for something in the garden. I sit in a blossoming tree to watch. And what do they find? Painted eggs!

Yancuic Xihuitl

Now I fly away, far and wide, all the way to Mexico! The Aztec people, who spoke the Nahuatl language, built great stone pyramids here over five hundred years ago. Now in spring, many people of Mexico celebrate March 11th and 12th, which are New Year's Eve and New Year's Day on the ancient Aztec calendar. There is singing and dancing to the beat of drums and people offer seeds in celebration. Candles glow and light up all the colorful costumes of the dancers. They wear brilliant headdresses of feathers from the sacred quetzal bird. Some play seashells like horns to make loud sounds celebrating the new year of life, just as the Aztecs did so many centuries ago.

Earth Day

And now I have traveled a long, long time, visiting spring celebrations all over the world! I saw dancing and music and picnics and parades. I saw people celebrating the sun returning to their lands, and Mother Earth growing seeds for new crops after winter's dark. I saw people celebrating flowers and trees, and finding freedom, and remembering light and joy with laughter and play. I saw so many ways to celebrate the gift of new life and joys of spring.

Now I fly one more time around the world—on Earth Day! April 22nd. All over Earth, north and south and east and west, I see people at parties singing and dancing and celebrating our home! And they agree to help all the new life come back to our Earth every springtime.

I help, too, and fly to my nest to take care of the eggs!

Activities

How many of each of these can you find in this book?
Look for them in the pictures!

Birds   Eggs   Flowers   Mothers   Seeds

Which one is in the most celebrations?

Birds   Eggs   Flowers   Mothers   Seeds

Can you find any other things that are the same in some of the holidays? Things people do? Or wear? Or eat? What are they?

What is your favorite thing about spring? How do you like to celebrate? Can you tell a story about it? Or draw a picture?

Can you point to every place I visited on a map of the Earth? Can you see where the equator is?

Pronunciation of Holidays

Noruz.................................NO-roo-z

Passover............................PaeS-oh-vuhr

Gelede...............................GEH-leh-deh

Kolla Raymi Killa.............. k-oh-l-l-ah R-EYE-mee k-ih-l-l-ah

Wattle Day........................wah-tl d-AI

Sakura Matsuri..................SAA-Kuw-Raa mah-t-SOO-r-ee

Chun Fen..........................CH-when f-uh-n

Basant Panchami...............b-us-uh-n-t p-uh-n-ch-m-ee

Holi ....HO-LEE

Easter ....EES-tuhr

Yancuic Xihuitl..................yah-n-koo-ih-ch SH-EE-w-ee-t

Earth Day ....ER-th d-AI